"You have one life to live, what do you want?"

Cindy Bahadur-Ramkumar

Some of the best compliments received:

"I like the theme Changing U……you are looking and doing good….I am proud to know you……" M.B.

"…Just look at the mirror and smile at you because you are an amazing person and no one else can do what you do…" R.L.

"I know you mentioned dress code in your book, I will try to change, now I look forward and up instead of look at the ground….." R.L.

"I need someone's opinion so I can learn from it, and I think you are the right person to get it from…." R.L.

"..Amaaazing…." K.L.C.

"…I had to admit it's the 3rd time that I am repeatedly reading your family acknowledgements!! I love it!!! …" G.E

"……You have given me the confidence to keep pushing myself to better and brighter things in my life. Thank you very much Cindy; May God continue to bless you as you seek to build up others around you…" G.C

"…Reading this book was a real eye opener, I want to thank you *for this book so easy to read and the stories so simply put, but has great impact on those who will read it. If any person reading can only just pause for a minute they can peep into the windows of so many others who have their curtain drawn, as they themselves look around at their space. Thinking what do I do and where do I go from here. This book is massive, it is not overbearing, but powerful in the stories presented because it is real!..." M.L.*

"....Thank you again for being a Keynote Speaker at our event. We greatly appreciate it....." M.S.

"...and your book is WOW! Absolutely, Absolutely Amazing!!!! What I learnt from your book, I could have never done on my own. NO one teaches anything for free. I promise you I will continue to share my experience with everyone about your book. I highly recommend your book to anyone who is lost as an entrepreneur..." M.R

"....After your advice about getting a notebook and scrap book, and making your own business card and flow chart of my plan, I try to believe it's not too late and its actually possible to believe in myself again....." J.C

"...You go girl, keep on doing your thing and making us women proud. It's an honour to know you...."M.L.R

"......I got your books last night; they are so easy to read and make me think...".I.B.

> *"Stop and take a chance*
>
> *to*
>
> *appreciate life."*

Cindy Bahadur-Ramkumar

CHANGING U

IN 101 WAYS

Author

Cindy Bahadur-Ramkumar

Copyright © 2016 Cindy Bahadur-Ramkumar

CHANGING U IN 101 WAYS

All rights reserved.

No part of this publication may be reproduced, stored in a retrieval system or transmitted, in any form by any means, electronic, mechanical, photocopying, recording or otherwise, without prior written consent of the publishers, author and copyright holders.

The author and publisher have made every effort to ensure the information contained in this book was correct at the time of going to press and accept no responsibility for any loss, injury or inconvenience sustained by any person using this book.

All contents of this book are the author's professional opinion; the author recommends you must seek legal advice when managing your business, company organization, your personal and professional life.

ISBN - 10: 1535407956

ISBN - 13: 978-1535407953

DEDICATION

Dedicated to everyone struggling to find a change in life, desperately wanting change, and uncertain how to attain it.

Dedicated especially to my mom *Angela Bahadur*, a pillar of strength, who learnt in the most unfortunate way, to adjust to a life-threatening change imposed upon her versus willingly wanting to make a change.

Dedicated to every single parent in the world, it's a tough, sometimes thankless, no love job, that never ends even after the kids grow up. But you made it, we all made it, changed and sacrificed our lives for our kids.

Dedicated to every person in this life who has faced some sort of abuse; physical, emotional or mental. Abuse at the hands of an abuser has the tendency to break your spirit and break you, scarring you forever. Never let the abuse *Change U*

Dedicated finally to my sister *Indira Bahadur* and my dad *Ramchand Bahadur*. Miles apart but I know you have my heart forever.

"The only path to changing my life

is

to change

me."

Cindy Bahadur-Ramkumar

ACKNOWLEDGMENTS

Thank you to each person who has touched my life, shared their life with me, and helped me in my journey to bring this book to fruition. I consider myself blessed to be included in your life, to be asked to contribute to your success and to share your burdens.

Sometimes, a person just needs a listening ear, someone to listen to them, and someone to share their thoughts with. A lot of times, we hear but we do not listen.

Thank you again to everyone who assisted me and helped me in this journey to put together CHANGING U.

Finally thank you to my two besties (Alezandro – my daily dose of nagging and Milano – my book manager, proof reader and editor), my sweetheart (Onalin – you keep my stress level in check) and my fav person in the whole world (Neal). Your strength and belief in me is colossus and undeniable.

*"Trust the process,
the results will reveal itself,
only
if you trust."*

Cindy Bahadur-Ramkumar

Foreword About The Author

CHANGING U, is written by Cindy Bahadur-Ramkumar.

Cindy is a Change Management and Management System Consultant, having worked in the field of Management and Change Management since 1998 (more than fifteen years).

Cindy has perfected the art of Change Management for personal self and professional life, by working with private, public, state-owned and non-profit organizations.

Cindy understands change, the cultures associated with change, the frustrations with change implementation and the personalities of those who oppose change and those who are fearful of change.

Cindy has implemented change management systems both in professional and personal lives of her clients and customers.

> *"Ask yourself,*
>
> *does that help you grow?*
>
> *If it doesn't,*
>
> *stop doing it immediately."*
>
> Cindy Bahadur-Ramkumar

FOREWORD ABOUT THE BOOK

- Are you tired with life?

- Fed up of life?

- Mentally and physically exhausted?

- Do you feel like every time you make one (1) step of progress, you make ten (10) steps backwards?

- Do you just want a change, a new life, a second chance to make things right?

- Are you tired of living in someone else's shadow?

- Have you ever felt that life keeps moving at a fast pace, but you are not going anyway. You feel like you are swimming in a circular pool, with no visible end in sight.

If you answered YES to all these questions, then this book *CHANGING U*, was written for you. *CHANGING U* takes you on a journey to be the best you, you can ever be.

CHANGING U, shows you in *101 Ways*, how to find you and make a better YOU. Change is a very difficult path to take in your life, however once you take it, you will never turn back.
I am very proud of this book.

This book started out as a scribble (jot notes) on a notepad. I thought about ways people can change their behaviours to become a better person. I have studied and observed human nature for the past fifteen (15) years, particularly looking for, what I call "drivers" which cause changes in a person's professional and personal life.

I began documenting in point format the "drivers" and the avenues to being a better "you" by examining the problems and providing the alternate solutions. I was not interested in the problems people encountered, as much as I was interested in the change solutions and outcomes of enhancing personal and professional problems. What started out as a scribble of points on a piece of paper, became a detailed list of changes to be used to implement change within you and your surroundings.

The transition of change management is very fascinating, starting with a particular situation and arriving at a specific outcome. The transition in-between is always the hardest and most difficult to conquer, as people are not readily apt to change their behavior or environment.

CHANGING U, is about changing everything about you to become a better human being, a more grounded, purposeful human being, a human being with solutions to problems and a human being that appreciates life, a leader and not a follower. It's about implementing a change from within, from deep down inside of you, while working on your outer shell and preserving the inner beauty, to perfect that beauty and leader to be YOU.

"I trust in my abilities,

no one else except me knows my true capabilities."

Cindy Bahadur-Ramkumar

"Begin by changing your circle of influence; this includes friends, peers, colleagues and co-workers."

Cindy Bahadur-Ramkumar

Let the Changes in Your Life Begin From Today

1.
To Acknowledge

The first step to changing you is:
- acknowledging that you have a problem
- acknowledging that you need help
- acknowledging that you cannot do it on your own
- acknowledging that with help, everything becomes easier

Acknowledgement and acceptance of your current situation is tantamount to changing you. You must start off by acknowledging your current situation and realizing that 'this is what it is, there are no do-overs and no extras". Accept and acknowledge your current situation. Acknowledge this is "where

I am today", and be willing to move forward from today. Willingness to change is the next step to begin the change management process of changing you. You have to be ready and willing to change you. Willing to start the process of changing you to be a better, different person. Willing to move forward and not look back on your life, but move forward into the uncertain.

2.
The Situation

If you can't change the situation change you;
- change your approach to the situation
- look for other, more simplistic ways of doing the same task
- change yourself to be out of the situation
- find a solution to your situation and make the change

Your situation would not change unless you change you. Your situation is the current environment within which you operate, function or reside. It could be your home, your workplace, your place of worship, your school etc. It is the current place which makes you sad, depressed, uneasy, uncomfortable, and you no longer have joy going to that place. It was once a livable place, however the environment is no longer conducive to your happiness. Acknowledge that the current situation does not work for you and be willing to change you out of your current situation.

3.
Curve Ball

When life throws you a curve ball, play the curve ball, hit it with all your energy and inner strength that you have inside of you. Make sure that you hit it out of the park, to a far off distance, ensuring that your opponents never return to the field. Play that ball as if it's the first and last ball you will ever hit. Curve balls are like meandering corners on a road, a lot unknown and uncertainties exist behind every corner, but give it your best shot each and every time. Don't let any curve ball distract you from your true goals.

4.
Circumstance

You either change your circumstance or change yourself to exit your circumstance. Only you know your real circumstance and environment within which you live. No one else knows your true financial, economic and personal life. No one knows your mental frustration and state of mental depression. Others could never feel your pain and know of your burdens and problems. Begin by making a decision to change you, adhere to and follow through on your decision. If your personal or professional environment is not conducive to enhancing and improving the quality of your life, make a concerted decision to exit your circumstance.

5.
Make a Choice

Make a choice and move forward, do not harp on or spend time on items and situations which consume your energy and may never change or improve. Human beings have the tendency to be afraid to make choices and decisions because of fear of its outcome. At some point or the other, you will have to make a choice to live in the moment, live the best life you will ever live, and be the best person you can ever be, for you, not for anyone else, be the best you can be for you.

6.
Vulnerable

Be able to expose your inner self and open your soul up to vulnerability. Being vulnerable is the scariest feeling in the world. Vulnerability shows your pure and exposed self, and allows you to subject yourself to judgement, opinions, critique from others. Vulnerability strips you of your protective self and forces the world to see you for who you really are (a beautiful soul, desperate to be free), rather than who you pretend and mask yourself to be. Being vulnerable helps you manage your fears and inhibitions. It also opens doors for you which would normally be closed, because you were afraid and fearful of the unknown.

7.
One Day at a Time

Live life one day at a time. Greatness happens one day at a time. You cannot really appreciate life, its simplicities and its benefits, if you are not living it one day at a time. Indulge yourself in life pleasures and its intricacies one step at a time and one day at a time. It's an indulgence, you will savorly enjoy. Changing you, means being able to appreciate life's blessing daily, regardless of the blessings being big or small. Appreciation of simple pleasures is the key to finding, peace, joy and happiness. Appreciation also displaces your feelings of anger and hurt. Change you by appreciating what you are blessed with and being grateful that you can live life to the fullest, one day at a time.

8.
Let Go of Mediocre

Resist the temptation and stop accepting mediocre, when you know you deserve greatness. I never truly understand why the human race settles for and accept mediocre on a daily and constant basis. Our response to mediocre is "it is ok, I can work with that or it is ok, it will do for now", when we know deep down inside of us, it is not ok. It's as if we don't even know our true standards and have no idea how to adhere to our own standards. Accepting mediocre means you are directly and indirectly allowing mediocre to be your norm. You will never be able to attain more than mediocre, if you don't give yourself a chance to experience greatness. Greatness is not accepting mediocre.

Changing you means letting go of mediocre to allow greatness to enter your life.

9.
Begin With You

Begin the change process with you, no one can change you except you and no one is allowed to change you except you. It's unfortunate when we feel the world owes us something and everything; because of the misfortune we were born into, the abuse we were subjected to, the poverty we were born into and the bad, unfortunate people we met along the way in life. The world does not owe you or me anything. The reality is, no one can change your situation except you. You have to begin your own change process, it has to start with you. Don't expect the world to change your situation, but accept that you have to begin to change you by first starting with you.

10.
One Task at a Time

Undertake one task at a time. The human mind can realistically only undertake one task at a time. In a world where we are told to multitask (doing many things at one time), our mind can only focus on one task at a time. To ensure that the task is completed in its entirety, we should focus only on that specific task. Jumping from one task to the other does not help you to achieve your goals, in fact, you end up with multiple incomplete (half-way done) tasks, which you may never get completed because your personal interest in completion would have wavered and disappeared. One task at a time, should be the only goal of changing you and enhancing your completion status check sheet.

11.
The Moment

Live in the moment and cherish the moment. Imagine living in a world without moments. I think it would be a very meaningless existence. Moments create memories, memories fill the void, the void will no longer exists with moments. One of the best parts of changing you as a person, is living in the moment. Once you are able to capitalize on "the moment", you will better be able to enjoy life and enjoy every moment of life, appreciating all that life has to offer. Living in the moment, means that you are fully enjoying and treasuring every aspect of your life and appreciating every milestone that you achieve. Moments = Appreciative life.

12.
Understand and Accept You

Begin by accepting you for who you are and who you have become. The initial part of changing you is understanding who you are. It is very difficult to change you if you do not know who you are or what's your purpose. Understanding you as a person, is a very tedious, complicated and confusing, sometimes teary task. Accepting you as a person is much easier. Begin by accepting you, embracing all your faults, your flaws and your insecurities. It is sometimes very difficult to accept you as a beautiful person, when the mainstream media bombards you daily with the opposite image of beautiful. The mainstream media portrays beauty as "flawless without imperfection".

Embrace and love yourself with all your flaws and imperfections, you are special, you are unique, you were handpicked and made a special way, because you have a special purpose and contribution to the world. You will only be able to understand and appreciate you, if you accept you for who you are. Acceptance and understanding of who you are, is foremost to changing you.

13.

Close the Doors

Close the doors to pieces of your life that are filled with pain, hurt and unpleasant emotions, and begin to open new doors which create joy and contentment. Sometimes when people hurt us or we are hurt by life, we hang on to the hurt as a means of defense, to say to the world "look at me, I was hurt, I need your comfort, sympathy and empathy". In order to move forward with your life, those doors that contain the hurt and pain need to be closed immediately. Keeping the memories of hurt and pain alive and active in your mind, stirs up discord, disdain and resentment within your being. Learning to close the doors, to forget the pain, to seal it away forever, allows you to heal faster. It also allows you to fill your mind with happy moments. New doors create joy and excitement, old doors expose pain and suffering. Choose your doors correctly and choose the path you want to follow to change you. Close doors that are no longer worthy of remaining open, and keep it closed forever.

14.

Your List

You can only change you if you acknowledge firstly the items about you that need to be changed. Make a list of all the items that you need to change about you. Some changes may be about your financial situation, your personal family life, your work life, your social life, the manner in which you mentally think about yourself, your commute to work, your lack of material things etc., and begin by working through each change, starting with the easiest change first and working towards the hardest and most difficult to change last. In order to perfectly execute change, you need to visualize it on a list which you can refer to daily.

The list created is the most effective method of visualizing change for you. You should list every item that you need to change about you or improve in your life. Physical properties of your appearance should not be on your list. List only items which will make you a better you. You will realize that you have an exhaustive never-ending list. Begin with the items that are the smallest and easiest to fulfill. As you begin to complete each change, your list will become smaller and smaller, after a while you should not have any items to add to your list. You should then start adding dreams and aspirations to your list once you have completed all the items that you want to change about you. You will have a new list of items you would like to achieve and attain success in. Changing you by utilizing a list is worth every effort, agony, pain and tears.

15.

Change Out

We have been mentally conditioned to accept our current environment. We do not know any other environment except the environment which we are subjected to and reside within. If you are not able to change the environment which you are currently residing in, begin by changing you to fit into your environment. Adapt to the culture of the environment you reside in (survival mode), until you can make a better move and change your situation. After which you should begin to change out yourself from the environment which you do not belong. This change out may take some time, however you should not give up. Change out yourself to be the real you and the best you, you will ever be. Change out your environment that you and your personality out-grew, and seek out the new and unknown. Changing out begins with you realizing that the environment within which you reside is no longer befitting to your persona.

16.

Leave

The most difficult and hardest decision you will ever have make in your life, is to leave your current situation. Part of change management is understanding that change is sometimes uncomfortable, uneasy and most feared. As scary as the thought to leave might be initially, ask yourself, what else do I have to lose? If you have lost everything else in life, and there is nothing else to lose in this life, except your dignity, make the decision to leave. The only recourse to live a peaceful, more meaningful life is to leave, leave the environment which makes you unhappy, helpless and feeling alone. Leave the world that has inflicted pain onto you, resentment and hurt, leave the world that has made you cry daily, leave the world that has scorned you, and embrace another world that will accept you. Be patient, the world will accept you. You are beautiful.

17.
Defined Achievable Goals

Each day ensure you have defined achievable goals. Goals which you are able to achieve every day and you pride yourself in achieving. Goals create purpose. Living a life without goals is like swimming in a circular pool. You are just swimming around and around and around, with no exit point. Having achievable goals means you have a purpose, you have something to live for, you have something to wake up to everyday and you have something to achieve every day. Define your goals and start achieving them.

18.
Get Up and Get

Don't expect the world to feel sorry for you because you feel sorry for yourself, get up and get, get up and provide, get up and take care of yourself. Self-pity is the worst form of begging, expecting the world to feel sorry for you because of your unfortunate circumstance. You need to seriously change you and your approach to life. Stop feeling sorry for yourself and your misfortunes, get up and get what's needed to take care of yourself and your family. The more you attempt to help yourself, the more you will realize the world is actually helping you without you knowing. What you give to the world you will receive, help yourself and the world will extend a helping hand to you in ways you least expect it.

19.

Take Control

When you feel that the wheels of life are spinning out of control, you need to find it within you to take control of the steering wheel of life and steer your life into the path that it was intended to take. Life is a journey and you are the driver of your journey. The road may be winding at times, uphill, downhill, and around corners. You need to fully understand that the only driver in your journey is you, if you do not take control of the steering wheel of your life, you will soon spin out of control. Out of control leads to chaos, problems, disagreements, mistrust and all negative thoughts and actions. Control your steering wheel before it spins out of control.

20.
Stop

Stop feeling sorry for yourself, stop expecting the world to feel sorry for you, and stop expecting the world to provide and care for you. The world doesn't owe you anything, in fact you owe the world. You owe the world to be a valuable citizen that contributes to the up-liftment of society and mankind. You may be able to convince some people your problems are never-ending, plagued with disaster, but after a while, people will slowly forget and ignore you, as soon as they realize you are being selfish and expecting the world to pay for your misfortune. Come out of your sorry state and start contributing to society. It will make you feel better about yourself and your life.

21.
Seek

Seek out a mentor, seek out someone who is an expert in the field of expertise; that you are desperately trying to get into, or would like to enhance your current skillset, and become like a "sponge". Soak up all that goodness, all that mentoring, knowledge and expertise, the tricks of the trade that made them a success. Ask to shadow them, and learn, learn, learn. You are never too old to learn. Once you have mastered their knowledge, find your own style and be the best you can be at developing your own style. Do not forget to help change someone else's life by sharing your knowledge.

22.

Be Confident

Be confident in your abilities, confident enough that, you understand:
- who you are?
- what you are about?
- where you want to go?
- how you need to get there?

The best part of changing you, is growing and enhancing your confidence in your abilities to excel at any task you undertake. Your confidence will take a while to build, but once built, there is no person in the world can take it away from you. Confidence is one of those unique characteristics that enhances every part of your being and leads you to be the best you ever will be.

23.
Own the Stage

Own the stage, own the spotlight, own your space, as if it's all yours and you deserve to be on the stage. I enjoy being on a stage, I enjoy imparting my knowledge and I own the stage because it is where I belong. I feel most at peace when I am in front of others imparting my knowledge. The best part of growing up is owning the stage and the spotlight. The stage is a beautiful place to be. It's also a very scary place to be. It's the place where all eyes are on you and everyone is looking up to you. The stage should always be your greatest achievement, it's the place where you will be judged, critiqued and empowered to do more. Don't be afraid to change you, to dream big and own the stage. Allow the spotlight to shine on you and embrace the light, it is where you belong.

24.

Appreciate

Appreciate the simple blessings and pleasures of life. Too often we are caught up and engrossed in a chaotic, confusing life, we forget to appreciate life's simple blessings. Our ability to breathe, our ability to walk, our ability to have a roof over our head and food on our plates are often taken for granted. We forget that we have really been blessed with lots; a bed, loved ones, kids, a job, a brain, clothing, freedom, security, human rights and safety. We are very quick to judge and critique others, and complain about our misfortunes, we forget our simple blessings we have in front of us. Part of changing you is changing the manner in which you look at life and changing the manner in which you relate to others and appreciate all that you have been blessed with.

25.

Learn and Create

Learn from others their about their success and strategies and create your own success stories. Life lacks meaning if you don't have anything to talk about or be proud of. If you continue throughout your life without any defined and known purpose, you will soon become bored of life, and question your existence. Emulate others, look at them, observe them, and find creative ways to learn about their successes, strategies and failures. Once you have studied successful people, find one person out of group you studied and begin to create your own success story by envisioning yourself as that person. Always ensure, whatever you do, you do it better than the person you emulated. Create your own niche and carve it out the way you dreamed of doing it, don't let others stop you from dreaming.

26.

Do

Begin to do, begin to make a change within yourself, and within your environment. The only person capable of making a change is you. Don't expect your environment to make a change for you or your friends and family to change you. In order to begin to change you, you have to start doing what feels right to you and what feels right for you. Only you can do for yourself, no one else can do for you. Make up your mind to do what's right and good for you, in your best interest, and don't leave it up to others to create your life for you.

27.

Let the Tears Flow

On days when you cannot go anymore and you cannot live anymore, cry. Let the tears flow, it's ok to let it out, cry as hard as you want to, as loud as you want to and as much as you want to. Let the tears flow and let the healing begin. The best form of healing is tears. Tears are the burdens overflowing from inside, when the mind, soul and body cannot bear with and handle life anymore. Sometimes tears are the best therapy. There is no therapist in the world who can heal you, as much as you letting your tears flow on your own. Free yourself and let your tears flow, it feels good afterwards and it is the best remedy for a broken you.

28.

Safe Spot

Find yourself a safe spot; find yourself a place where you alone can be you. My safe spot is in my vehicle. I get to be me in my vehicle, I get to cry, laugh, think happy thoughts and think about life. My vehicle takes me all over the country, and it's the only place that I am allowed to be me without being judged by others. I can cry for miles, and no one will notice, I can sing as loud as I want and no one cares, and I can let my mind wonder for miles into my trip and no one can disturb my thoughts. Find your own safe spot, a place where no one can judge you, a place where you are allowed to cry, scream, get angry and be happy with yourself. That's your safe spot, it is the only place where you can be you and are allowed to be you. Your safe spot is a place where you can be you, free from the world. It's the only place where you get to be you in a world that's yours without the interference of others.

29.

Pray

Sometimes when you feel that the whole world is against you, that the world is unjust, the world is unfair and that your life is tumbling uncontrollably, just pray. Whatever faith you are, whatever higher being and God you believe in, just stop and say a prayer. Ask for help. Don't be ashamed to ask for help. Ask God to lead and you shall follow, ask God to bare your burdens, ask God for a moment of smiles and a glimmer of hope. Praying gives you a bit of consolation that everything will be ok, and someone out there is looking out for you. You have nothing to lose and everything to gain, with a simple little prayer.

30.
Believe

Believe that you can make a change in your life and believe that you have the ability to make that change. Nothing is stronger than the belief that you have in yourself. At times your belief in yourself may dwindle, and you may doubt your own capabilities and abilities. However you need to pick yourself up, give yourself a pep talk, pat on the back and reassure yourself that all will be ok. The only person to believe in your capabilities and your abilities is you. No one else knows your true potential like you and no one else knows what's in your heart besides you. Your belief in yourself is more powerful than any words of encouragement offered by others. The only person capable of changing you is you. Make your beliefs real, powerful and actionable.

31.
Goals

Set a goal for yourself, a realistic achievable goal, and ensure you invest every ounce of your time to achieving that goal. The only path forward in life and the best path possible to changing you is to set realistic achievable goals for yourself. Goals are meant to assist you and help in defining what you want to achieve in life. Your goals must be realistic though, unattainable goals tend to discourage you from achieving them because they are just that; unattainable, unable to attain or reach. Make sure you set goals that you can achieve and know you can achieve. Put a timeframe to your goals, and discipline yourself mentally to achieve the goals. One goal at a time, one task at a time. Dream big, and dream realistic.

32.

Focus

Focus on the end and not on the beginning. Focusing on the beginning, forces you to spend time trying to get everything perfect from the beginning. Focusing on the end results, makes the starting details minute in comparison to the end result. We tend to get lost in and distracted by a project or task, because we are overwhelmed by the mere thought and complexity of the task. Redirecting your focus to the end result and the possible outcome, allows you to channel all your energies towards the end. Once you direct yourself to think of the end result, you are better able to manage the beginnings and in-betweens which may occur. Choose a task, choose a deadline and fill in the path towards achieving the task, making sure you keep your mind and all your efforts solely on the end result. It's like winning a medal at the end of a race, the medal is all yours because you worked towards it.

33.
Ask Yourself

Every task that you undertake, ask yourself how will it help me achieve my end result? If it is not helping you achieve your end result, drop the task and move on to the other task at hand. It is very frustrating to undertake tasks without clearly visualizing the end result. You need to question everything that you do;

- is it right?
- is it wrong?
- am I making money doing it?
- is it wasting my time?
- can it help me?
- am I in it for the long haul?

Question, question, question yourself, it's the only way to decipher right from wrong, progress from delay, wasting time or being productive. Questioning your actions, forces you to become accountable for your actions. Keep asking yourselves these questions, you are on the right path to changing you.

34.

Process

Devise a process to complete each task within a specified period of time. Things will never get done on its own, a well-defined plan and process helps gets tasks completed at a faster rate. Processes and flow charts are visual additions, which aids in the enhancement of your understanding that all assigned tasks need to be completed. Processes are generally considered as the underlying layers and foundations to a good plan. Every process has a beginning, a middle and an end. Create your process to achieve your end with accuracy and efficiency. The best part of changing you, is making sure you utilize processes available to you to achieve your desirable outcomes and results.

35.
Time

Put a deadline and timeline on every task before you begin it. Put a start date and an end date. Hold yourself responsible for finishing these items within the required date. Time is the most important, valuable resource you will have in your life. Once it's gone, it's gone, it will never come back. Every second, every minute, every hour and every day, becomes the past. Sadly you are not able to change the past, you have the ability to brood about the past, but you cannot change the past. Why waste the only gift that has been given to you for free, without a price tag or strings attached? You need to begin to visualize your time as valuable, your time as worthy and your time as important and needed. Once you reach that state of being where your time is of value, you are on the right path to changing you. Associate your time with goals, dreams, aspirations, and put a dollar value on your time. Whether you work for someone or work on your own, you salary is calculated hourly, employers pay you what they believe you are worth, or what they believe you can contribute to their business. If you don't perform any tasks for an hour, and sit idle, you have just wasted an hour of your time and you have not generated any income to substantiate that one (1) hour wasted. Put a value on your time, and begin to visualize yourself as someone whose time is of value and is valuable, not to be wasted.

36.

Hate and Love

Hate yourself to the extent that you are fed up of you and that you want to change you. Love yourself unconditionally, whereby your hate turns into love, because there is no more of you to hate. The only other option you have is to love you for being you. You need to have a love-hate relationship with yourself. You need to start hating everything that you do, that you abhor, detest and wish you could change. Hate the things you do not like about you and be willing to desperately change you. Upon reaching a state where you willingly want to change, you will begin to love yourself slowly and in tiny bits and pieces, to make you better. Don't expect anyone to have that love-hate relationship with yourself, except you. Only you can love you as much as you deserved to be love, and only you can hate you as much as you deserve to be hated. Out of hatred, always spawns love. Love means change.

37.
Want It

Want it so bad that you are hungry and desperate to make your life different, hungry for change, hungry to see yourself succeed. You cannot depend on others to want a better life for you, neither can you depend on others to change your current situation. Only you can change you. Wanting things in life is as unattainable as a fisherman throwing a line out in the ocean and wanting to catch the biggest fish. He can throw the line as many times as he wants and hope one day to get the catch, or he can want that catch desperately that he throws the line in the spots he believes he will get that catch, utilizing all the resources available to him (compass, net, boat, bait etc.). You have to desperately want things in life, desperate enough to be willing to change you, in a good way, to achieve everything you set out to achieve. Wanting things in life, should be like having a seed planted inside of you, a spark that has been ignited that you are more than willing to go out and achieve. Keep the spark ignited and the fire burning inside of you, want it desperately enough to change you, change your current environment and change your outlook on life in order to achieve it.

38.
Want-To

Create a "want-to" list. A list of things, actionable items and dreams that you want-to do to be who you are destined to be. I personally like a "want-to" list. It's a list of things that I want to do with my life. My list is in the form of a tiny pocket book. It's called my "You have one life to live, what do you want" list. Every day I write one (1) item that I want to do, and work towards achieving it. Your list can contain simple items like wanting to read, or ride a horse to as complex as wanting a house or a baby. Build your own want-to list of wants and work towards achieving your wants, "one want at a time".

39.

Dream

To change you, you need to have a dream. Dream big and pursue your dreams with determination. You have to ask yourself, what is this precious life without dreams? Life would appear meaningless if you didn't have something to look forward to. Dreams allow you to have purpose. Live your life as if you are in a dream every day and you do not want to be awakened, make it the best dream you ever dreamt, and have fun living it.

40.
Post It Wall

I personally love post it walls, and I have gotten my kids into the habit of using post it notes and building their own post it walls. I can't see my original walls because they are covered with different coloured post its from my kids, but I see the dreams, sparks and fire lit inside my kids. It's a compromise (of no visible walls versus a wall made up of post it sticky notes) I am willing to live this compromise. Buy yourself some "post it" labels, and write each item from your to do list on a separate post it note. One post it = One to do item. Create a "post it" wall by sticking each to-do item on your wall. Your wall will initially look congested and complicated. Every day, remove one "post it" from the wall and work away at the task listed on the post it note. Once completed, move on to another "post it". Soon your wall will become empty, because you will diligently focus on completing your tasks listed. You can also add some excitement to your post it wall by using various colours of post it, different colours mean variations of complexity. Less complicated tasks are yellow to most complicated task being red. I like red, it's a vivacious colour, full of life and passion. Change you by building your post it wall.

41.
Stop Complaining

Your worst enemy is you. You need to stop complaining about everything that is wrong in your life, and start appreciating everything that is good in your life. The more you appreciate you and the others around you, the less you would complain about you and your life's misfortunes. Begin by starting to appreciate life, and appreciate all that you are blessed with. Begin by being grateful and thankful for life's blessings, it could always be worse. Take a minute for yourself, look to your left, really look at the person to your left and then to your right, think about their misfortunes and their unfortunate situations in their life. Look at yourself now, and realize that you are a very fortunate person, your life could be far worse off than it is right now, turn your mindset around, and begin to change you by not complaining anymore.

42.

Time Out

You need to take a time out for yourself every day. The same manner in which a child is given time out, to sit, ponder and analyze their actions and consequences of their actions, you need to take a time out for yourself to sit and analyze your current steps and strategize your next steps forward, towards improving your current situation. Give yourself your own time out, lock yourself away from the world, forgive yourself for your wrong doings, and open your mind up to a world of possibilities. We all need time out, it's the best form of re-energizing ourselves and rejuvenating our inner soul. Time out is good for you, ensure you utilize the benefits of time out wisely.

43.

Willpower

Our biggest downfall is our inability to control our urges and complete things that we begin in life. In life, temptation will surround you all the time, the temptation to take a shortcut, temptation to not complete a task, temptation to follow a different route and temptation to break a commitment. You have to garner the willpower from within you (deep inside of your being – mentally) to not succumb to the temptation that's all around you. To have and maintain willpower is very difficult, even the best of us succumb to temptation. Mastering the art of willpower is a powerful feat and it comes from internal commitment to changing oneself from within. Be patient with building up your willpower, one day at a time, one task at a time, one step at a time. Take baby steps if you have to, but you will make it.

44.

Surround Yourself with Positive

The power of positive thinking is the most difficult of all changes, however it is the most rewarding. Positive vibrations, positive people, positive situations, positive conversations enhance your personal aura and mentally removes you from the negative within your life. Ensure that you surround yourself and engage only with positive people. Positive people emit and radiate positive vibrations, which directly displaces negative vibrations and fills your aura with good vibes. When you surround yourself with, and affiliate with positive people, you will not have any time to engage in negative conversations, opinions and situations. Positive people and situations will uplift your entire being; the mind, body, soul and spirit.

45.

Halo

Try your utmost best to ensure you create a halo of positive energy around you (you can create your positive vibration halo by surrounding yourself with only positive). Assume that you are enclosed within a circle and that no one can penetrate that circle. The circle is a "goodness halo", an area filled with positive energy, positive vibrations, positive thoughts and positive emotions. Do not allow anyone with a negative aura to contaminate your positive energy. Negative people walk around with negative vibrations. The more you maintain and control your positive aura, the more successful your undertaking will be. You will spend less time focusing on negative people and their negative attitudes and more time focusing on ways to enhance and better yourself. Build your halo and maintain your halo of goodness.

46.

Stop Worrying

Worrying consumes time and energy, depletes and exhausts you mentally. Worrying causes anxiety, irritability and mood swings. Worrying forces you to focus your energy on items and concerns which may not or cannot be resolved immediately. Stop worrying, it's not worth the time, effort or energy. Do not worry about the things you cannot change, focus on the things you can change to make you a better you.

47.

Be a Game Changer

I like being a game changer, I love change and enjoy being the change initiator. All successful people are game changers. They look at life as a game, and play the pieces of the games accordingly. To become a winner, you will have to play like a winner. You need to know your opponents every move and you also need to strategize you next move. Look at your life as a game. In order to win in this life, you have to win the game. Be a game changer in your life. Ensure that every move you make in your life, you are making a winning move. If the move does not benefit you, financially, mentally, physically or emotionally, then it's the wrong move. Plan again and change the game to suit you and your needs. Change your game to win.

48.

Regain Control of Your Life

You have to look at your life as if you are standing above, looking in, observing your every move. You will notice that your decisions are spinning you out of control, causing you pain and problems. Having the ability to take control of your life and direct your life along the life continuum, one step at a time, shows that you are able to take control of your life and propel it in the direction you want it to go. Before your life spins out of control, get a grip of it, grab the reigns and regain that control. Don't steer your life into an unbeaten path, steer it into the path where you have the most control. Pick up the pieces and begin to be you again.

49.

Push Pass Your Limits

Every day I push myself a bit more. Some days I am successful and other days I am not. I push myself to be the best I can be with the resources available to me. I extend my limit daily. Your body is only able to move as fast as you want it to move, your life is only able to proceed in the direction you propel it. You will know your normal limits and the extent to which you can push yourself normally. To know your true limits, the true extent to which you are able to propel yourself, you will have to push yourself past your current limits. Set unattainable your goals, reach outside your comfort zone and push yourself as far as you wish to be. Only you can define your limits and push past it.

50.

Overcome Your Story

Each person has a story. It may be having a life of hardship, prosperity, loneliness or success. We all have our own stories, that's the beauty of life. Each person has varied stories and varied backgrounds. We get to write the story we want, we just need to understand how to write our own story. Your life is made up of minute little stories which culminate into one giant story. Your story has molded you to become who you are today, the human being that exists within you, a body attached to emotions and materialism. Your story should never define who you are though, but rather contribute to your physical and emotional make-up. Whether you like it or not, your story changes every day, with each new encounter. Overcome your old story and create your own new story. Don't let your story define you, rather take some time to define your own story, your own beginning, middle and end, overcome your old story and create your new story with the new you. It is very exciting to write your own story. You can become the storyteller of your own life.

51.

Go All The Way

I have always found that life becomes meaningless if I don't go all the way. It would feel as if I gave up before it was the time for it to get some meaning, or the things that I was doing I did not have a vested interest in completing. The what ifs, should haves and could haves, seem to have a way to penetrate my mind after the fact and cloud my judgement, forcing me to give up, loose interest and be unhappy. The worst form of injustice you can inflict upon yourself is to not go all the way until the end. Many times, we as humans are willing to begin every new tasks presented to us, the excitement, fanfare and interest of a new task, catches our attention, however we soon lose interest and we never see it through to the end. We are our worst enemy, we find excuses and conceivable reasons, for not completing anything we started and never finished. To truly define who you are and to know your full potential and true capabilities, you need to go all the way until the end, until you achieve the desired result. Stop short-changing yourself, and try to do something good for yourself at least by finishing what you started.

52.

New Beginning

Every day you may feel that you need a break, you need some light in your life, you need just one more chance. You need to create your own new beginning. Sometimes, when life gets frustrating and you have given up, stop for a moment and think. Think about finding a solution to put an end to the chaotic nonsense that is taking place all around you. No one can create that new beginning for you except you. You need to seek out that new beginning, be it a new place, new job, new home, new start, new life. Only you can create your much desired new beginning. Try it, it's worth every tear that flows. New beginnings are amazing, it gives you the ability to be you again, a better more experienced you.

53.

Pain is Only Temporary

Pain hurts, it always does, if it didn't, it would not be called pain. The tears will flow, the pain will mentally exhaust you and physically bruise you, but it is only temporary. Condition your mind to believe that the pain you feel is temporary and it will all be over very soon. Remind yourself that "not everything last forever". Tears will never flow forever, and bruises may hurt, but the visual scars will disappear after a while. Mentally condition yourself to believe that pain is only temporary, it is the only way you will be able to survive your pain and cope with physical and emotional pain. Your situation does get better, one day it will. The light at the end of the tunnel is within your reach, you just have to extend your arms to embrace it, it is waiting for you.

54.

I Have a Purpose

You will feel like some days are unbearable, frustrating and confusing. You may feel lost, alone and lonely. You are living an empty life. A life without a purpose is a meaningless life. Until you find your purpose, life will continue to be meaningless. You will continue to roam aimlessly in this world of mundane existence. Every day when you wake up, remind yourself that you have a purpose, and by trial and error you will soon find your purpose. Find the one thing that brings you the most joy in this world, puts a smile on your face, you look forward to doing it, and you feel as if this is what you were meant to do with your life, this one thing is your purpose. Don't expect to find your purpose overnight, it won't happen. Do some soul searching, and find that one thing that gives you the most joy, happiness and contentment. If you are happy doing something, you will never look at it as a burden, you will always look forward to completing it and enjoy doing it. Find your own purpose and have a blast exploring it. It's important for your overall well-being.

55.

Define Your Own Self

Never let anyone define who you are, what you were meant to do and who you are supposed to be. Define your own-self, define your own capabilities, set your own threshold and be who you want to be. Don't define your life by the definitions and standards of others. Defining your self is the most controversial thing you will ever do to change you. One day your heart will lead you in one direction and another day you mind will lead you in the opposite direction. You will be torn between your heart and your mind. Your heart follows your dreams and aspirations, your mind follows practicality and reality. Find a way to strike the balance between your heart and your mind, your dream world (heart) and reality (mind). Reality means your bills have to be paid, it's now, in the moment, it's real. Dreams mean you live in a world where it takes longer to pay your bills, where you are building a platform to success. Define your own self and decide how to find the balance between mind and heart, reality and dream world. Define you, by understanding you and changing you by trial and error.

56.
To Grieve is to Move Forward

Give yourself permission to grieve, permission to cry, permission to let go, permission to express your hurt, pain and anger. Give yourself time to grieve openly, without worrying about what others think about you. Grieving is the best form of therapy, it allows you to let go of built up and pent up feelings, and emotions, in the best way you know how. We all grieve differently, no two persons express their emotions in the same manner. I might hold my grief inside of me and cry silently on my own time and in my own space, while you may want to express your grief in public and in the presence of others, seeking their comfort in the form of hugs and kind words. Grieve in the manner which feels the most comfortable. Grieving gives you the ability to move forward and the ability to let go at the same time.

57.

Increase and Enhance Your Vocabulary

Society judges us by the choice of words we use and the manner and eloquence in which we communicate. In order to appear coherent, eloquent, intelligent and to be able to fit in to any situation and conversation, you will need to increase and enhance your vocabulary. Read and familiarize yourself with the terminologies and lingos of the conversation which you perceive yourself contributing towards. Society rewards intelligence, frowns on dumbness, and looks down on lack of intelligence. It's disappointing to live in a society like this, and sadly it's the reality of the world that we co-exist within. Intelligent people fit in, they are appreciated, rewarded and placed on a pedestal. Non-intelligent people are treated like cast-aways, normally pushed aside or not given a second chance. Figure a way to enhance your vocabulary and the manner in which you convey your words. Make yourself sound and appear intelligent and eloquent.

58.

Make an Impression

Impressionable people are remembered, people who make an impression, people who stand out, people who grab the attention in an audience of many. If you do not make a personable impression, you will soon be forgotten, and not given an after-thought. Imagine being in an audience of 50 people, all with the same dreams and goals, only one person will be selected for the final prize. How would you stand out to obtain that prize? What would you do to capture the speaker's attention to get that prize? You have 10 seconds to create the most unforgettable impression, what would you do? In life, whenever you meet anyone, you should always leave the person you met, with the best impression and thought about you. Stand out, be unusual, be creative, be unforgettable. Align yourself with something to be remembered by, create ways for people to remember you and methods to associate you by.

59.

Command Authority

Most successful people command some type of authority. They assume leadership roles and create authority for themselves when none is present. You have to command authority to be able to be heard. The reality is, the world does not accept shy people. Hence the reason for the creation of training programs to allow shy people, (called introverts) to explore their personality and learn how to become outspoken and brave (called extroverts). Shy people are often unheard, not heard, quiet, silent voices that disappear in the crowd. If you want to be heard, you have to speak up, you have to own your space and you have to be an authority on the topic which you speak about. You must command authority if you want to be successful, in both professional and personal life. Create a reason for your voice to be heard, your opinion to be valued and respect to be given. It's all about owning your space and letting you presence be known. Learn the art of commanding authority and start owning the space that you believe is yours. Change you by taking control and commanding the authority your rightfully deserve. Be respectful, be authoritative, be kind and be forceful. Always make sure that you get the respect you deserve and that you are kind to others while on your journey of commanding authority. Authority and respect compliment each other and go hand in hand.

60.
Define Your Own Successes

Success has many, many definitions. It becomes confusing attempting to define the word success and define the achievement of success. Success to some people means material acquisition, while to others it means mental contentment. Only you can define your own success, set your own bars and standards and work towards achieving it. Create your own success bar, and devise a plan towards achieving it daily. Take some time out for yourself, really think about your own definition of success, then write it down on paper and reference it daily. Give yourself daily reminders of where you need to be and what you want to achieve. Does success mean attaining money, does it mean standing on a stage, does it mean helping the world, and does it mean leading others? You are the only person who can figure out your own definition of success, once you decide on your definition; you can begin working towards achieving your own success. Define it = Achieve it.

61.
Try Something New

Push yourself out of your comfort zone and try something new daily. At first it might be a bit difficult and uncomfortable, however, once you get into the routine of trying one new item daily, you will begin to look forward to daily new tasks. Try something new, it's worth the effort. I have personally found, when working with clients and customers, one of the biggest stumbling blocks to changing you is the fear you hold within. The fear of the unknown paralyses your thought processes and breeds fear into your mind. Fear of the unknown is the most difficult type of fear to overcome. As humans, we are very comfortable and capable of living within our comfort zones, accepting a mediocre life, when in our heart we know we deserve greatness. We have conditioned ourselves to accept mediocre as our greatness, we no longer know what greatness feels like. Don't be afraid to step out into the unknown and try something new. What is the worst that can occur if you try it and you don't like it? You will return to your comfort zone and be afraid of trying again or you may want to try something else, because the one you tried didn't work. Try something new, commit yourself to trying something new every day. Try one new item, one new task, one new food, one new trip, one new act of kindness. Help make you better by trying something new every day. Trust yourself, it is worth it in the end.

62.

Trust in Your Capabilities

No one knows your capabilities except you. You are destined for greatness and to be successful, however you have to trust in your own abilities and capabilities. Trust in your own strength and your own abilities. No one knows you as much as you know yourself. How many times in life have you been told, you are not good at something, you cannot do it, it's not for you, you are not worth it, you are worthless? Deep down in your heart you know you are destined for greatness, but no one else can see it, because you are never given a chance to prove your greatness. Trust in yourself, only you know your true self, only you know your limits and capabilities, only you know you. Stop allowing others to decide your capabilities and strengths, stop allowing others to create your you, and stop allowing others to dictate your potential. If you believe you are worth it, and you believe you have the capabilities to be who you believe you can be, go after it, and don't let others stop you. Prove others wrong, by trusting in whom and what you believe you can become.

63.
Strength in Leading

There is strength in leading others, strength in numbers and strength in the ability to assume leadership. The more you assume the role of leadership in your personal and professional life, the more you are better able to learn from your mistakes and make calculated, concerted decisions, in the interest of your team. The success of a team depends on the strength of its leaders. Leaders have the ability to lead their team to greatness and to success or to failure. As a leader, you automatically assume the role of knowing what to do, and when to do it; you assume the role of a winner. Start looking for leadership roles, or create your own leadership roles, whereby you can build your strength and knowledge in leading. People respect leaders, they respect a leader's ability to lead the team to success and a leader's ability to be strong and committed to the end.

64.
Live the Life

In order to become what you were truly meant to be, you have to live the life of your imagination. Begin by planning your own destiny and your life's path. You can live the life that you are destined to live in a very methodical manner, if you believe you can and have faith in your own capabilities. To be like your role model, your mentor, your idol, you have to create the persona that gives you the ability to live the life that you are dreaming of. You cannot be a superstar if you have never been exposed to the superstar type of life, or be a model if you have never seen the life of a model. Start preparing yourself mentally to live the life of which you were destined to live. To be a superstar, start making yourself known in areas where you believe superstars frequent, be a volunteer or ask for a job there. Make yourself known and make yourself available. Find creative ways to start living the life you were meant to live.

65.
From Now On

Everything from now on, moving forward in your life must be perfect. Live each day striving for perfection, and indirectly eliminating imperfections in your life. Only strive for excellence. I personally like the phrase "from now on", it gives me the chance to start again, the ability to begin all over and the ability to leave the mistakes and past behind. From now on, you get to be who you want to be, from now on, you get to live life one more time, from now on, the past can never haunt you and from now on you are given one more chance. Live life each day as if you are starting anew, and create new memories, new successes and a new you.

66.
Be Hungry

People eat for two reasons; either they are hungry (stomach is empty) or there is an innate desire within to consume a food item. Live your life as if you are hungry; hungry for learning, knowledge, money, material items, success and peace. Make sure you have a burning hunger inside, within you, willing to change you, in the same manner you have a burning desire to eat and consume food when you are hungry. Be hungry for change, be hungry to change your current situation and be hungry to conquer your life one more time. Hungry people are driven to find food, when you are hungry in your life, you become driven to find the real you.

67.
Define a Strategy

You must have the ability to create a strategy to be successful. You need to take some time out for yourself, gather your thoughts and write on paper a defined strategy to enact your success. You need to have a plan and a strategy to succeed. By not having a plan for yourself, you have already set yourself up for failure. If you study the behaviours of successful people, you will understand, all successful people have plans, all successful people enact their plans and all successful people live life by achieving their strategic goals. Have a plan, define your strategy and go after you own success.

68.

Prioritization

Changes and life situations have the tendency to constantly bombard you. Changes in your life are taking place all the time. Many changes tend to cause confusion and you become lost and frustrated. Start prioritizing your tasks, from the least important to the most important. Begin by working away at the most important tasks and ensure these are completed within a reasonable timeframe. When you begin to complete each task, look for high priority tasks, and treat them with some level of urgency. These need to get done first. Prioritization eliminates chaos and brings closure to outstanding matters. Prioritize what's important, work on it, and move on to the next.

69.
Passive Aggressive Dictatorship

You have to be willing to change your approach to your personal and professional life, whereby you adopt a different type of lifestyle which steers away from a passive aggressive controlling type of life. You have to become actively involved in your life, be more assertive and firm. Steer away from being aggressive and authoritarian, and channel your focus towards a democratic, assertive, active approach to life. Passivity breeds complacency, aggressive breeds anger and dictatorship breeds upheaval. Adopt an active assertive lifestyle, which makes you actively involved in changing your life, without bringing discord and contempt, but rather respect and partnership.

70.

Communication vs Engagement

In order to enact change from within, you need to engage respective parties involved in the process. Sometimes, this means involving all parties by utilizing the engagement approach, where everyone has a value added opinion about a process or a change, rather than communicating from above and on the outside. Often parties that communicate with others never really impart information effectively. Communication is different from engagement. Engagement means having parties actively involved, soliciting input and opinions, communication means imparting information, sometimes from a position of authority. As it pertains to applying this principle to changing you, you should ensure that you engage others when imparting information, so that you receive active constructive feedback to make you a better person. Always engage others when you communicate.

71.

Results Oriented

Transformation is the result of changing you and your approach to life, whether it is your personal or professional life. Adopting a result oriented approach to every task that you undertake will yield results inevitably in a positive way. A result oriented approach holds you accountable for your assigned tasks and pushes you to complete items within a specified deadline. You are driven by results, and driven by your ability to succeed. The more positive the outcome and results, the more you would want to move forward and achieve. Part of changing you is accepting that there is transformation taking place in your life and positive results enhancing your transformation. Keep on achieving results and keep on transforming. Self-transformation leads to a better you, a better you makes you happy, which becomes visible in your demeanour.

72.

Utilize Resources Effectively

The world is full of abundant resources. These resources are at our fingertips for utilization. We tend to become entwined and engaged in life and its problems that we forget to utilize the resources available to us, or we utilize the resources, but never really utilize it effectively. Effectively means making the best use of what is given to you. Changing you means utilizing the resources available to you in the most effective manner, making the best use of what you have available to you. Do not let time pass you by and regret that you did not have a chance to use what was provided to you. For example, you currently have your health; you are a healthy individual, save for few pains here and there, why don't you capitalize on the fact that you are healthy, you have both arms and both legs, your organs function and you are mentally able; and really do something with your life rather than sit down and expect life to give to you. I cannot over-emphasize how much utilizing resources available to you effectively is important to changing you, all the resources are available to you, use it wisely and effectively to make you a better you.

73.

Change Culture

Culture is significant to the success of change management and changing you. How things get done around here or the culture, impacts the change and the manner in which change is executed. You have to change your mental culture, change your innate culture and change your environmental culture, only then will you be able to change your culture and the manner in which things get completed. Culture is a mindset, a mindset which dictates your approach to how you get things completed. Change your approach to how you see life, change your approach to how you perceive life and change your approach to how you want to fit into life. Your cultural mindset allows you be a better person or a worst of person. Your cultural approach helps you integrate into society, the world of work and your personal life. Always try to manage your changes and try to fit into each workplace's culture, and the culture of the world. Cultural fit is extremely important to your current and future success.

74.

Informal Leaders

Sometimes being an informal leader allows you to change your approach and mannerisms in life. While you will strive to be a designated leader, an informal leader or a person that rises to the occasion and takes ownership and responsibility, garners just as much kudos, respect and praise as a designated leader. When given the opportunity, always strive to lead. Leading brings out the best in your personality, and drums up a world of respect for you from others. An informal leader is best type of leader, people often look up to informal leaders. Informal leaders take initiative and take control of situations. Informal leaders take risks, take chances, and gain the respect they deserve, allowing them to change themselves in the process of being better.

75.

Environment

A coherent environment needs to be created, "I get it, I know what I need to do to make this happen". In order to change you, you need to make your environment work for you to your advantage. Not every environment is conducive to success, however the manner in which you make things happen in your environment, creates success. You can look at your environment and think it's not conducive to change or you can look at your environment and believe that it can change. Environments don't make people, people make environments. People's mindset is conditioned by the environment within which they reside and operate. Change your environment and change you in the process.

76.

Hard Work

Being a disciple of hard work and the hard work regime, working hard is the only path that takes you to success. Hard work in this book means, applying yourself diligently to any assigned task and ensuring that the tasks are borne to fruition and completion. Hard work is not meant to be referenced as laborious work, or work that is intense and manual. When speaking about hard work, I am speaking about applying yourself diligently and dexterously to any task that you undertake. Make sure that your hard work pays off and that you are rewarded handsomely for your valiant efforts. Never let your hard work go unrewarded or un-noticed. Hard work and dedication breeds success. Work hard and work smart.

77.

Work Smart

The solution is always within reach, however the approach is sometimes questionable. If you can resolve your approach to a certain task, you are indirectly forcing yourself to work smart. Smart workers utilise a resolution based attitude towards problem solving and are able to move on at a quicker rate to another task than a regular worker. Working smart means that you are working in the interest of completing a task effectively and efficiently. Working smart means you try to meet and exceed the expectations set out in the task, you try to supersede the deadline and finish before the intended date. Working smart also means that you are not wasting your time on other tasks which may distract you, and that you are eliminating the wastage of products and processes within your task. I have always heard the saying "work smart, not work hard". I feel both terminologies complement each other, you need to work both smart and hard, smart enough to finish before your intended deadline, and utilize the resources efficiently and effectively with little or no wastage. Work hard by applying yourself diligently to your task, to ensure it is completed with little or no room for changes, additions, or deletions.

78.

Start Acting in a Certain Way

Start acting in a certain way to enact change. The only person to enact change and change from within is you. Your friends, co-workers and family cannot change you. They may want the best for you, they may want that you live a very fruitful engaging life. As much as your family and friends want a better life for you, your life will not change unless you begin the change process yourself. Start acting in a certain manner, a manner which befits the role you are assuming. If you want to be a business person, start acting like a business person, if you want a life away from burdens and worries, start building your life where burdens don't consume you, if you want a life away from abuse (verbal, emotional, physical), start acting as if you are not being abused. Once you get a taste for the life that you desire and dream off, you will no longer accept the life that you have or the life that was imposed upon you. You will begin to build within you, a sense of determination and drive to succeed, to be who you want to be, and nothing will stop you from changing you and being you.

79.

Engage Others

Engaging others in your dreams and goals, helps keep you accountable to achieving your dreams and goals. Align yourself with people your trust and ignore the naysayers. Always make sure the engagement is fruitful, honest and constructive. Choose wisely and include only those who truly want to see you change, grow and succeed. One of the best forms of achieving success is having someone hold you accountable for your actions. Make sure you choose someone who truly wants you to succeed and is genuinely interested in your success. Maybe you want to live a peaceful life, maybe you want a life full of rewards and successes, maybe you just want a life of a human being to be treated like a human. You can achieve any life you want, the world is your platform to perform on, you need to engage others so that they hold you accountable to your dreams and actions.

80.
Celebrate Successes in Moving Towards the Goal

Never forget to say thank you. You didn't climb the mountain of success on your own and you will never be able to conquer further mountains on your own, without acknowledging where you came from and how you got to be where you are today. Always say thank you, to those who assisted you along your way to become who you have become today. Two simple words – thank you – open doors that have been previously closed for you. Recognize and acknowledge the persons who have touched your life and assisted you along your journey to changing you. Allow them to celebrate your successes with you, and ensure that you create a separate pedestal to put them on (not literally, but in thought). The more you celebrate your successes, the more favourable your future successes will be. Don't forget to be humble and kind in everything you do. Humility opens the doors of success and closes doors of hatred and animosity.

81.
Refuse to Accept Second Best

Mentally position your mind to believe you are the best and reject offers that are subpar and below your standards. Never accept that you are second best to anyone, or inferior to anyone, based on gender, sex, race or education. You are the best at what you do, and believe that you are. Human beings have a tendency to belittle others to make themselves look superior, it's a characteristic of our human nature that sorely stands out. Never let anyone make you feel inferior to them. Never let anyone hold power and control over you. You are the best at what you do, and the hurtful words of another human being should never penetrate into your mind to make you feel that you are second best to them. Be the best that you can be, so that second best becomes a figment of your imagination. Change you by being the best and not second best.

82.

Adapt

In order to survive in any environment, you have to adapt. You may have to adapt mentally, emotionally and physically. If you don't try to adapt and fit into your environment, you will soon make yourself uncomfortable in the environment, and force yourself out of the environment which you are desperately trying to fit into. Picture yourself as an ocean fish swimming in a fish bowl. An ocean fish is free and swims the ocean without restraint. An ocean fish living in a fish bowl is confined, frustrated and in need of freedom. Unfortunately the ocean fish may never get to swim in the ocean again due to its fish bowl limitation, however the ocean fish can adapt to be the best possible ocean fish in the fish bowl. The point is, make the best of any situation bestowed upon you, and learn to adapt and change you to fit into that situation. It may not be the most ideal situation at the present time, however in the future, the situation may change. You have a choice, sit and brood over things you cannot change or make the best of things you can change and look forward to a brighter future.

83.
Make a Choice

You cannot go about your personal and professional life "sitting on the fence". You need to make a concerted choice and move forward. Sitting on the fence, not making a decision shows an indecisive personality, it shows a person who is afraid to make decisions about their personal or professional life. Make that choice and move on. Make the choice in the best interest of all parties involved including yourself. Life is about choices and decisions. Not every choice or decision will give the desired intended outcome, however you have to make a choice and move on. Make the best possible choice given the situation you are in, and move on. Part of changing you is making a choice and moving on.

84.

If You Look for Negative, You Will Find Negative

Some days you will find yourself feeling defeated by life, you will find that you can't go on anymore, that you have failed and you are just about to give up. If you look for negative things and moments in your life you will find the negative. If you focus on the positive improvements and accomplishments in your life you will find positive. You need to choose your focus and not let your mind focus on the negative. Stay away from negative people, they tend focus only on the negative things in their life, and make you feel depressed. Invite positive people into your life, people who are willingly able to contribute to your positive success. Leave the negative people at the doorstep of your life, do not allow them to enter your life.

85.

Let Go of the Noise

All around you there is noise. From the time you awake in the morning, until the time you close your eyes at night. Noise can become tedious and mentally draining. The constant clatter and noise that consumes daily life can become exhausting, it mentally drains you and exhausts you to the point where you cannot deal with it anymore. Letting go of the noise is one of the changes you need to make in your life to change you. Free up yourself from clatter, chatter and noise. Walk away from the noise, remove yourself from the environment where the noise is becoming a nuisance. The more frequent you remove yourself from the noise, the more comfortable you become with not tolerating the noise. Let go of the noise and open yourself up to calm, peace, quiet and a new you.

86.

Have an Unbreakable Spirit

Your inner spirit and soul will drive your changes within. Your spirit needs to be rock solid and unbreakable, you cannot let people and situations break your spirit. You have to make sure your inner soul is strong and that you constantly know your purpose and your meaning of existence. You will find that the devil will play games with you constantly and bring unhappy, contagious and negative people into your life, people who have the ability to drain you mentally. Keep your spirit strong and make sure your barriers are high enough that these people do not contaminate your spirit and break it. The stronger your spirit, the more difficult it is to remove you from your purpose in life.

87.

Create Your True Legacy

One of the best and most valuable reason for living is to be able to create your true legacy. After all, in each of our lives we have a beginning, middle and end. The two most definite things in life are the beginning (birth) and the end (death). The in-between is uncertain. The in-between is the blank canvas given to you. It is blank, it has absolutely no writing on it, no paths to take, no decisions to make. Your job in this life is to create your true legacy or that part of your life that you want people to talk about after your passing. Instead of letting life pass you by every day, and becoming frustrated by lack of progress and stagnancy in life, figure out a way to create your true legacy. Define the words that you want to be remembered as "selfish, stingy, kind, harsh, abusive, educated, intelligent, mean, hurtful etc." What image do you want the world to remember you as? Only you have the ability to paint your own canvas, only you can create your true legacy. Leave something behind for the world to remember you. Your legacy is what you will leave behind when you pass on (die). What do you want people to converse about when they talk about you? What's the mark you will leave in this life that you will be remembered by? Finding your true legacy takes a while, but once found, it makes life more meaningful and livable. It is an extension of your purpose, which makes your life more beautiful and fruitful.

88.
Light the Fire

Light the fire in you to open yourself up to more. You may become complacent sometimes and get fed up of life and its progress. You have to constantly keep the fire of life and purpose lit inside of you. Once that fire is lit, the flame will become brighter and brighter as you allow yourself to feel and experience more and more in life. Open yourself up to more, experience life and experience the world. Keep your fire burning and never allow it to extinguish. The brighter the fire, the stronger your purpose. Feed the fire, provide it with fuel, and keep it lighting forever.

89.

Turn a Song into a Performance

Life is about performances. We perform every day of our lives. The spotlight is directed towards us each and every day. Make every performance the best you can. Do not leave room for critique. People remember you when you turn your life into a performance. If the most talented musical singer stands on stage and sings, without any performance, people will soon forget the song and the singer. That is a forgettable singer, it means the singer has not had an impact on the audience. If the singer gives it their best and moving performance while singing, people will remember, because the performance was unforgettable. Live each day as if you are performing for an audience with an unforgettable performance. Leave a good impression on people's mind when they meet you. People tend to remember performances, make sure your performance every day is the best performance of your life, perform every day as if the world is watching you and the spotlight is on you daily. Turn your day into a performance.

90.

Tell Your Story Slowly, Then Explode

Let your life be like a story book, one page being read and told every day. Each of us has a story to share about our own life. Life is a story. We have become story tellers of our own lives. This journey in life is your story, and you get to tell the story with your ending. Our life is a like a book made up of mini-chapters. Each chapter has a specific reveal. Tell your story piece by piece, give others a glimpse into your life but hold off until the climax. Make sure your audience wants to hear more and more of your story daily. One day your story will climax, and the world will see you for being as beautiful as you are, but until then, slowly reveal your story and keep the world waiting and wanting more of you.

91.
Have Fun

Always have fun doing what you love. If you are not having fun, then you are not loving what you are doing and it is not for you. Only you can decide if you are having fun. The best measure of doing what you love and loving what you do is examining your level of your passion, your thoughts, indulgences, and your fun meter. When you are doing something that you love and are passionate about, it becomes fun for you. You will always smile while doing it, you can't stop thinking about it, you definitely enjoy it every day, and look forward to doing it. You should live life like you are in a marriage to your passion, you have fun every day and you can't live without your passion.

92.

Keep Your Audience in Suspense

I like intrigue, I like suspense and I like to have fun. Slowly keep your audience in suspense. Whatever you do, do not provide the beginning, the middle and the end of your story all at once to anyone. Your life is your story, make sure you are the best story teller to tell your story. Never let anyone tell your story for you. Take the reign and be the best storyteller of your life. Suspense breeds anxiety and anticipation. People are fascinated by success and determination, be wise when you are sharing your story. Not everyone needs to know everything about you all at once and not everyone is genuinely interested in sharing your successes. Let your suspense reveal itself slowly and gracefully.

93.

You Only Get One Chance to do it Right

You never get more than one chance to do it right. The world is an unforgiving audience. One mistake and the world remembers you forever. Make sure you use your one chance wisely. If you do make a mistake, seek forgiveness immediately from the world and right your wrong. Your relationship with a loved one is like an unbroken plate, it is round and whole. If it breaks, it can never be whole again. No matter how many times you try to glue the pieces together, the plate will never be round or whole again. Make sure when you are using your one chance, you are always doing it right. Don't leave room for judgement, don't leave room for argument and don't leave room for mistrust. You only get once chance in life to make it right and a broken plate can never be repaired, so don't let your plate be broken.

94.

Humility Opens Doors

I learnt this trait from my mom. She was always a very humble lady. Being pomp and pious breeds disrespect, jealousy and hate. Humility breeds acceptance. Always remember humility opens doors. The more humble you become, the more people respect and admire you. The world respects humble people. Cocky, self-conceited people never get very far in life, they find a way to burn their bridges on the way to the top. Once they arrive at the top, the top becomes very lonely. Be humble and respect everyone along your path to success. You might need one of those persons one day to assist you further and they will remember your humbleness and willingly help you, and they will never doubt your intentions as genuine, because to them you are always genuine and humble.

95.

Open Your Mind

While the mind may be one of the most powerful parts of the human body, the mind can also be one of the darkest parts of the human body. You have to be able to open your mind to visualize the world around you. Do not allow your mind to trap you and hold you back from becoming the real you. Your mind can place you in an uncomfortable, depressed, lonely state, where you live in your own world feeling that there is no escape, or the only escape for you is to depart this world. Open your mind and explore the possibilities of the world. Free yourself from the burdens you mentally carry. Look around and realize that you are truly blessed. Life could always be worse off, but for now life is good. Free your mind to believe the world is a good place to reside, it's not as bad as your mind is telling you it is.

96.

Fix You

No one in the world can fix you except you. You may have been hurt in life, unexpectedly or willfully. The pain is sometimes visible on the exterior and hidden on the interior. While you may "put on a good face" every day, towards the world, you are the only person hurting inside. The only way to move forward in life is to fix you. As much as you want to hate the world and hope that the injustice meted out to you is duly punished, you cannot move forward unless you fix you. The first part of fixing you is realizing that you could not change the circumstance meted out to you. The second part of fixing you is letting go and realizing that you cannot control that which was dealt to you. The best part of fixing you is accepting that every second and minute that goes by, becomes the past, and you get a chance at a new start, if you are willing to take it. You are of no good to anyone, not even your kids, if you do not take care of you first. Fix you to be a better you. Let go of the past, it has no place in your future and it has no right to rob you of your future.

97.

Have Faith

Faith is tantamount to changing you. You need to believe in something or someone. Believe that there is a higher power watching over you. Believe that the higher power is taking care of you. Believe that you are being cuddled by hands filled with love, believe that someway along the journey of life, there is someone up above watching you and ensuring that you live the path intended for you. Believe that when you cannot go on anymore, and you are about to give up on life, there is someone walking beside you, waiting to catch you when you stumble and lead you again on your path. Trust in someone, trust in a higher power, trust in yourself that you will make it out of the rough patches in life. Have faith in yourself and trust that the changes taking place in your life are meant to change you for the better.

98.
Be a Child Again

Don't be afraid to be a child again. Children are the most innocent of the human beings; their minds are like a clean/blank slate "tabula rasa", clean and untouched. Children's mind and thought processes are often influenced by their environment and their interaction with adults. If the environment is negative, the child will grow up with a negative mindset, if it's a positive uplifting environment, the child will grow up seeing positive in life. Children normally enjoy life and are free spirited. Children are the most innocent beings of this universe, their minds are truthful, honest and never tainted. Children don't know hate, they only know pure and honest love. You should live life as if there is no tomorrow, laugh like it's the first time you are laughing, and smile at a silly memory of you every day. Visualize your world as if you are watching it through the eyes of a child, pure and with innocence.

99.

Top of the World

Live on the top of the world. The world is actually a very beautiful place from above. Position yourself to view your world and the world you live in from above. Escape to the top of the hills and mountains, if you can, take a deep breath and enjoy the view from above. It's a beautiful world when you look down at it, and the best part is, this beautiful world can be all yours, if you just believe that it is yours for the taking. It's yours to conquer, it's yours to succeed in, it's yours to shine and be the best you can be. Make the top of the world yours and enjoy the view from above.

100.
Always Have the Last Word

Unless you are in a disagreement, you should always have the last words in any conversation. People remember last impressions and last words. Make sure your last words and last impressions leave the best impression of you. Let your words be kind, be courteous and create the impression that you want people to remember you by. Last words are very powerful if used resourcefully and intentionally. Create your impressions by having the last words and ensuring that you are remembered.

101.
Be You in This Journey

At the end of all the changes you read and applied to change you, from the entire book of *Changing You in 101 Ways*, you need to be you. Be you, and never let anyone design your life for you, never let anyone help you lose your individuality. You don't have to like everything that someone else likes. Neither do you have to please everyone in this journey of life. You should always "want to" rather than "have to" do something with your life. Be you and only you. Unearth the inner and outer you, and allow yourself to shine to the world. Let the world see you as you were meant to be seen. Never hold back on you, give it your all, and enjoy every second and moment of the change that was you. Be you in this journey called life, laugh as loud as you want, shine as bright as the brightest star, enjoy every moment of your transformation and have fun changing you. Keep on Changing You to be the BEST YOU.

"The world is a beautiful place, you just have to open yourself up to the world.

Cindy Bahadur-Ramkumar

ABOUT THE AUTHOR

Cindy Bahadur-Ramkumar is the author *of 101 Ways To Think Like A Business Person* and *The Struggle is Real* and *Changing U.*

Cindy is also the CEO and Founder of Management Systems & Solutions.

She has built and taught businesses how to operate, sustain and grow exponentially on zero (0) credit, streamlined and consolidated businesses, coached businesses how to maximize efficiencies and reduce cost all while maintaining a PROFIT.

Cindy is well known for creating structure in chaotic business environments while implementing strategic process improvements.

She imparts the know-how on how to aspire to have your time equal more profit (time = more profit) and how to achieve profitable status as a business owner.

Cindy is extremely knowledgeable, experienced and

versed in continuous improvements, organizational excellence, change management, key performance indicators (KPI) and maximizing efficiencies.

Cindy is a Linguist, Management System Auditor and Consultant (HSSEQ - Health, Safety, Security, Environment, Quality) by profession, and is an Author, Reporter, Writer, Facilitator, Lecturer, Business Coach and Mentor.

To enhance your business potential visit www.mssconsultants.com and email cindy@mssconsultants.com

"Believing you can change is half the battle, completing the change is the remainder of the battle"

Cindy Bahadur-Ramkumar

Author
Cindy Bahadur-Ramkumar

Your Change Notes

www.ingramcontent.com/pod-product-compliance
Lightning Source LLC
Chambersburg PA
CBHW070239190526
45169CB00001B/231